Famous Firsts   Famous Firsts   Famous Firsts   Famous Firsts

Acknowledgments

I would like to thank everyone who helped me put all the pieces of this book together. It was a blast to get to speak with some of the firsts themselves, such as L. R. Herkimer, Banana George, George Nissen, Rick Twomey, Cory Coffey, and Bob Haro, who all helped me get the facts straight. I also would like to thank the various experts in their fields for reading through many drafts and donating photos. Thanks to my surfing experts: Neil Harrington, guest curator of surfing culture, Daytona Beach Museum of Arts & Sciences; Barry Haun, curator/creative director of the Surfing Heritage Foundation; and surfer Kurt Januszyk. A cheer for cheerleading experts L.R. Herkimer, father of cheerleading; Brandy Corcoran, University of Oklahoma cheerleading coach; and author Natalie Guice Adams of the University of Alabama. A shout-out to musher DeeDee Jonrowe and Iditarod education director Diane Johnson for helping with the sled dog section. To Carole Lowe, curator, Water Ski Hall of Fame & Museum, and Lynn Novakofski, graphic designer, USA Water Ski, for their countless hours tracking down photos and rereading the water skiing chapter. A jump up for George Nissen, trampoline inventor extraordinaire; Lani Loken, executive director, International Trampoline Industry Association, Inc.; and Paul Parilla, vice chair of the Trampoline & Tumbling Program of USA Gymnastics, who helped with the trampoline section. To Phil Kennedy, co-author of *Flat Flip Flies Straight*, and Wham-O Public Relations for helping out with the flying disc section. Thank you to Craig Snyder, writer and photographer, and Leslie Kovalic, archivist, Makaha, LLC, for their knowledge of skateboarding. To John Swarr, writer/director of *Joe Kid on a Sting-Ray*, Rick Twomey of Rick's Bike Shop team, and Cory Coffey, BMX pro, for answering my many questions about BMX. To Lorin Holmes, snowboarding instructor, and Marty Bodell, snowboard collector, for helping me with any and all snowboarding questions I had. And to Nicholas Skally, marketing and PR manager, Rollerblade USA, and Jason Hines, Competition and Demo Events director, for helping out with the in-line skating section. Finally, a big thanks to my editor at Lobster Press, Meghan Nolan, who helped me to keep digging deeper and finding tidbits that would have otherwise been left buried. This book is definitely the result of a team effort! – *Natalie Rompella*

Famous Firsts: The Trendsetters, Groundbreakers & Risk-Takers Who Got America Moving!
Text © 2007 Natalie Rompella

Published by Lobster Press™
1620 Sherbrooke Street West, Suites C & D
Montréal, Québec H3H 1C9
Tel. (514) 904-1100 • Fax (514) 904-1101 • www.lobsterpress.com

Publisher: Alison Fripp
Editors: Alison Fripp & Meghan Nolan
Editorial Assistants: Faye Smailes & Nisa Raizen-Miller
Book Designer: Lynda Arthur
Production Manager: Tammy Desnoyers

Library and Archives Canada Cataloguing in Publication

Rompella, Natalie, 1974-
    Famous firsts : the trendsetters, groundbreakers & risk-takers who got America moving! / Natalie Rompella.

(My America series)
For ages 8-12.
ISBN 978-1-897073-55-1 (bound)

    1. United States--Biography--Juvenile literature. I. Title. II. Series.

CT217.R65 2007   j973.09'9   C2007-901128-4

Printed and bound in Malaysia.

Wakeboarder cover photo courtesy of AWSEF Water Ski Museum/Hall of Fame

CONTENTS

INTRODUCTION

Surfing, cheerleading, sled dog racing, water skiing, trampolining, flying disc throwing, skateboarding, BMXing, snowboarding, and in-line skating all have Americans moving. But what else do all of these sports have in common? They all started in the United States!

Imagine being the first to invent a whole new sport or an original move. All of these inventions started with a simple idea, but over time, that idea became more complex. Sometimes that first thought morphed into something completely different. Each of the sports in this book started off as a brainstorm out of left field that someone took the time to perfect and then share with the world. But how did these people come up with their ideas in the first place? The answers might surprise you!

Did you know that …
- the sport of flying discs, popularly known as Frisbee, began with a lid from an old popcorn tin?
- the first cheerleader was a man with a plan?
- in the 1700s, surfers used to hang ten on 100-pound trees?
- some of the first homemade skateboards were made out of apple carts or dresser drawers?
- snowboarding was set in motion in the middle of a Minnesota snowstorm when a young girl wanted to surf?

Read on to learn more and find out which activity began with a barrel and which sport was inspired by the delivery of medicine. You'll see how some of these totally crazy ideas turned into totally amazing sports.

First Things First
Many people can do these activities with the proper equipment. Of course, you're going to read about star athletes, such as skateboarding legend Alan "Ollie" Gelfand and BMX star Cory Coffey, who perform risky jumps, flips, and grinds. These moves are done by professionals with proper training and supervision.

But the sports themselves can be done at different skill levels, and by kids – that's how pro Scot Breithaupt, who was considered one of the founders of BMX at the age of 13, Bob Haro, an 18-year-old inventor of many BMX tricks, and Lisa Andersen, who was a pro surfer by the age of 17, all got their starts.

You may notice that sports normally thought of as "America's pastimes" aren't included. The sports featured here are less conventional and continue to grow in popularity. They may not be shown on Monday night TV or sell out huge arenas, but they are still evolving in new and exciting ways, thanks to all of the inventors and their brilliant plans put into action.

Have you ever thought up a great invention, only to discover it already exists? Or maybe you've tried to find out who the first person was to come up with an idea, and different sources gave conflicting information. It's not always easy to track down the first people to have done something or where an activity began. Not all inventions are rooted in one specific location either. Although the sports in this book have strong ties to America, they had help from other countries too; for example, the dogs used for sled racing often came from Asia, and the skates that inspired the sport of modern in-line skating came from Europe. However, the sports themselves are considered American creations that have exploded worldwide.

So who were these trendsetters, groundbreakers, and risk-takers who got everything started? You might be surprised to learn they were regular people who had a desire to try something different and do something fun. They asked the question "What if?" and found the answer.

Now, let's get to the action! By the time you finish reading, you just might be inspired to create a "first" of your own.

Ride the Waves

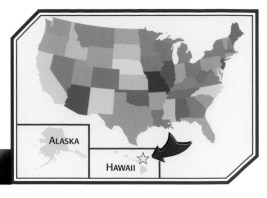

Long Before Surfing the Net ...

Surf's up, dude! Did you know that surfing has been around for hundreds of years? Hawaiian cave paintings of surfers may date back to the 1500s. Many years later, in the 1770s, British voyager and astronomer Captain Cook traveled to Hawaii to explore the land and found the island natives balancing on waves with boards made from trees. Hawaiian natives of all social classes (both royalty and commoners), as well as both men and women, surfed for enjoyment and sport.

As suggested in this early drawing, natives surfed both standing up and lying down.

Bishop Museum

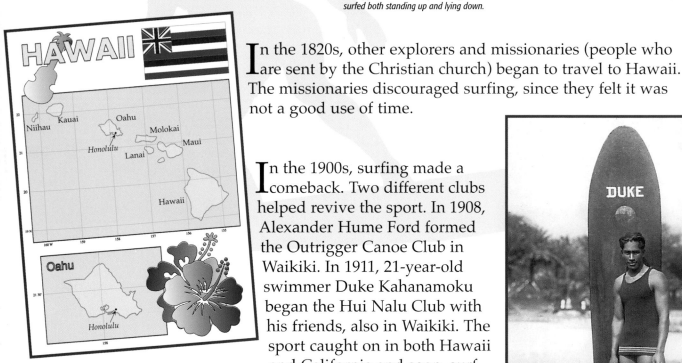

Hawaii is a group of islands. Some of the favorites among surfers include Oahu and Maui.

In the 1820s, other explorers and missionaries (people who are sent by the Christian church) began to travel to Hawaii. The missionaries discouraged surfing, since they felt it was not a good use of time.

In the 1900s, surfing made a comeback. Two different clubs helped revive the sport. In 1908, Alexander Hume Ford formed the Outrigger Canoe Club in Waikiki. In 1911, 21-year-old swimmer Duke Kahanamoku began the Hui Nalu Club with his friends, also in Waikiki. The sport caught on in both Hawaii and California and soon, surf lessons were in demand.

California and Hawaii are still the most popular places to surf in the United States today.

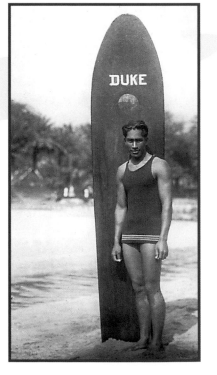

Duke Kahanamoku helped teach people in Hawaii and California how to surf. Here he is in 1912 with his surfboard in Hawaii.

Bishop Museum

During the early 1900s, surfboards were made of solid wood from trees, such as California redwoods. The boards weighed around 100 pounds. In the early 1930s, surfer Tom Blake patented a hollow surfboard. Because it was lighter, it was easier to carry, which allowed more people to surf. He later added a fin to the board, which helped with steering and angling. By the late 1950s, wood was being replaced with foam and fiberglass, which were lighter still and could be shaped more easily.

Tom Blake was the first to create a hollow surfboard, take photographs while surfing, add fins to surfboards, and write a book exclusively on surfing, called Hawaiian Surfboard.

Bishop Museum

Skimboarding starts on the shore, where the surfer waits for the right wave to approach. When it does, the person throws the board across the sand toward the water, jumps on it, and attempts to ride the wave back to shore.

A longboard.

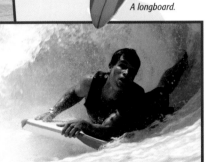

Like stand-up surfers, bodyboarders can also ride the tube, or inside, of a wave.

Boards are now made in different sizes, depending on the tricks or stunts to be performed. For instance, longboards (which are usually more than 9 feet long) are used for smaller waves and by beginners, since they are steadier than a shorter board. Many seasoned surfers also enjoy surfing on longboards. Shortboards (around 5 feet, 8 inches to 6 feet, 10 inches long) are harder to stand on but better for trick riding. Bodyboards, or boogie boards, which became popular in the 1970s, are small boards that people ride while lying on their belly.

Professional surfers have their boards custom made just for them.

Fun boards (seen here above on the right) are shorter than longboards (shown above on the left) but larger than shortboards. Fun boards are usually between 7 and 9 feet long and are best to use when the waves are smaller.

Three skimboards.

"Ready? Okay!"

What better way to raise team spirit than with a chant! Princeton University is credited as having one of the first football chants in America. "Sis, Boom, Ahh!" is what the students reportedly yelled out at an 1860s football game. It is thought that Thomas Peebles, a Princeton graduate at the time, may have brought the idea of chanting across the United States to the University of Minnesota. In 1898, as these two schools played each other in football, University of Minnesota freshman Johnny Campbell and five other men yelled out a chant to get the crowd going as Princeton had in the 1860s. The University of Minnesota Men became known as the first cheerleading squad.

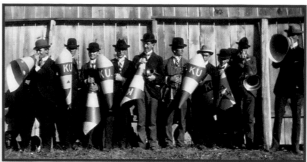

Spirit and cheer squads began as a way to get the crowd pumped up. This is a spirit squad from 1899.

University Archives, Spencer Research Library, University of Kansas Libraries

Longer and fuller skirts for cheerleaders were popular in the 1920s and 1930s. Skirts were made shorter during World War II because fabric was needed for the war.

In the 1900s, a national cheerleading fraternity called Gamma Sigma began. This gave men an opportunity to be recognized as a group on college campuses. In the 1920s, cheerleading saw two changes. Gymnastics became part of the sport, and women became involved, mostly in the form of pep squads. It wasn't until the 1940s that women began to dominate the activity. When men were drafted in 1941 for World War II, cheerleading was left open to women.

According to a 1939 *Time* magazine article, cheerleaders were judged by Gamma Sigma on the following: the crowd's reaction to the cheer, the moment when cheerleaders chose to begin a cheer, and the tricks they could perform. There were three specific tricks that were judged: the Ritter Span (a back flip with a twist, invented by Andrew Mowbray Ritter, who broke his wrist while attempting it), the Nelson Arch (another type of back flip), and Duos (in which more than one person tumbles in unison). The team that best demonstrated these skills was awarded by Gamma Sigma the title of All-American Seven (seven, because most squads had seven members).

The cheerleading uniform for men in the 1930s was usually a sweater with the team emblem on it, and a pair of pants.

University Archives, Spencer Research Library, University of Kansas Libraries

In 1948, L.R. Herkimer made a name for himself in the world of cheerleading. With his skill in gymnastics, he made his Texas high school and college cheerleading squads. After cheering for Southern Methodist University in 1949, Herkimer started up the National Cheerleaders Association. Not only did his association offer classes on gymnastics and cheerleading moves, it also made sure cheerleaders learned how to speak in front of others and create quality cheers, written with the help of an English teacher. Now, thanks to Herkimer, cheering camps are held all over the world to help cheerleaders work on their skills.

Herkimer was a cheerleader at Southern Methodist University in the late 1940s. He's on the right in the middle layer of this 2-2-1 pyramid.

National Cheerleaders Association

Herkimer doing his famous Herkie jump.

University Archives, DeGoyler Library, Southern Methodist University, Dallas, Texas

While at his camp in 1957, Herkimer found a squad that, although not the most skilled, had great team spirit. He pulled a branch off a tree and gave it to the team members. He declared it a spirit stick. This tradition continues today at cheer camps. Sticks that are red, white, and blue are awarded to squads with great spirit. Herkimer is known in cheerleading circles for something else as well: the Herkie Jump, named after him. To do one, a cheerleader jumps into the air and kicks one leg out to the side while the other is tucked underneath.

Trivia Time

One of the symbols most often associated with cheerleading didn't shake its way into cheerleaders' hands until the 1950s. Before this time, cheerleaders waved balls of paper streamers (referred to as "shakeroos"). While watching a troop of majorettes spin metal batons, Herkimer noticed that the batons didn't show up on the latest piece of technology – the color TV. He thought that adding colorful paper streamers to the ends would help make the batons more visible. The idea took off, and in 1953, he and his wife created the Cheerleader Supply Company, which sold these colorful paper pom-pons. They came in a pom-pon kit, equipped with crepe paper, wire, and a stick to hold on to, as well as instructions. In 1965, Fred Gastoff invented pom-pons made out of vinyl – a more practical material.

One of Herkimer's friends convinced him to patent his idea for the paper pom-pon, which he did in 1971. The patent (right) shows that cheerleaders would need to cut out their own crepe paper strips using a stencil. The Herkimers also sold cheerleading uniforms, including his wife's new design: the pleated cheerleader skirt, which could be made in school colors.

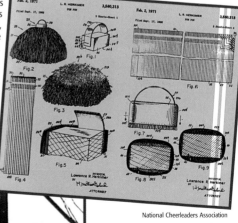

National Cheerleaders Association

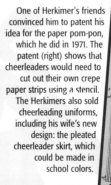

Herkimer sold more than 1 million sets of his paper pom-pons. Seen here is a cheerleading squad holding paper pom-pons in the early 1960s.

University Archives, Spencer Research Library, University of Kansas Libraries

One of the most famous cheerleading squads is also one of the first for the National Football League – the Dallas Cowboy Cheerleaders. In 1972, the manager of the Dallas Cowboys realized that the football games were more than just sport – they were entertainment. He chose to replace the high school squad that cheered for the team (the CowBelles and Beaux). He hired models to stand on the sidelines to add glamour to the game, but the heat got to them. He then decided to hire jazz dancers who had better stamina versus the models who were used to sitting still for photo shoots. He found a dancer, Texie Waterman, to run the tryouts, and 60 women showed up – seven made the squad. Waterman changed the focus of their role at the games by having the girls dance more than chant. It was a success.

Seven dancers made up the first Dallas Cowboys cheerleading squad. Since 1972, there have been only six changes to the classic uniform, including a modification in the style of boot.

Dallas Cowboys Cheerleaders

The types of pyramid formations have changed through the years. Because of safety concerns, cheerleaders can no longer do "3-high" pyramids. This squad is from 1979.

University Archives, Spencer Research Library, University of Kansas Libraries

In time, cheerleading, which started out as a way to support a sport, ended up being one itself. In the 1980s, cheerleading competitions began, and new jumps, flips, and stunts were created. The activity was no longer simply about chants and getting the crowd excited, it was about the choreography, balance, acrobatics, and teamwork. Cheerleaders not only performed at games, but at state and national competitions where they were judged on their ability to synchronize their moves and chants, on the level of difficulty performed, as well as on their smiles.

Herkimer created the National Cheerleaders Association in 1949. Today the organization holds national competitions throughout the United States, with tens of thousands of participants each year.

Moves such as basket tosses require spotters to ensure a safe landing.

American Cheer Star

Every Sport Deserves a Cheer

Although cheerleading started as a man's activity, 97% of cheerleaders today are female. In addition to football games, they cheer for field hockey, volleyball, and wrestling. These days, many high school and college cheerleaders' schedules have doubled. Some schools require cheerleaders at an equal number of boys' and girls' sporting events. Cheerleading, which began with six men cheering at a University of Minnesota game, has become so popular that now the number of cheerleaders in America could fill that stadium 80 times!

Cheerleading requires athleticism and flexibility. Here, cheerleaders perform pike jumps.

The scorpion is a difficult move that should only be attempted with proper cheerleading training.

Amy Johnson

Look Before You Leap

As with all athletes, cheerleaders risk injury. There is a proper progression for learning difficult moves so that muscles aren't strained and bones aren't broken. Before people can attempt certain jumps, tumbling combinations, or stunts, they need to have mastered the basics, such as tuck jumps (jumping up and bringing the knees in toward the chest) and round-offs (doing a cartwheel with the feet meeting at the top of the handstand and then ending with the feet together). Gymnastics and pyramid stunts also require qualified adult supervision, strong skill, teamwork, and communication so that no one gets hurt.

★ **"I was the first** to be on the cover of *American Cheerleader* Magazine."
– Penny Ramsey –

American Cheerleader magazine

Former University of Maryland cheerleader Penny Ramsey Otwell was also a Survivor (Thailand) cast member.

13

Race a Sled Dog

Working Dogs

For thousands of years, dogs all over the world have helped us work. Until the 1930s, brave sled dogs and their human owners delivered mail to remote parts of the Arctic. Sled dogs also helped their owners hunt and fish. They even carried migrating families across the Bering Strait from Russia to North America as early as AD 900.

Courtesy of Candy Waugaman

Mail delivery by sled dog in Chitina, Alaska, in 1916 (above).

Dogs were also used to haul heavy items, such as wood (as seen here). In the 1950s, sled dogs were replaced with snowmobiles.

Archives, University of Alaska Fairbanks

Miner Mushers

Gold! In the late 1800s, more than 3,000 risk-takers trudged north to Alaska and the Yukon Territory of Canada in search of gold. There were no cars or airplanes, so gold miners used dogs to pull loads of supplies needed for panning the creeks and rivers. If the miners were lucky, the dogs helped take home a load of gold. The sleds the dogs were attached to were made from local lumber like birch, ash, or hickory, and were tied together with moose hide or braided twine. The person on the back of the sled became known as the "musher." (The term comes from the French word *marcher*, meaning "to walk" or "to march.") "Mush" became the command for the dogs to begin pulling or to pull harder.

The winners of the first All Alaska Sweepstakes, musher John Hegness and his team.

Archives, University of Alaska Fairbanks

Let's Race!

Sled dog racing soon caught on as a pastime, but rules needed to be set before it could be a true sport. In 1907, Albert Fink of Alaska helped start The Nome Kennel Club – the first organization to arrange sled dog races. The club held the first official race in 1908. The All Alaska Sweepstakes ran from Nome to Candle over 408 miles of tundra. It took 100 hours to finish!

A couple of years later, investor and sled dog musher Charles Fox Maule Ramsay from Alaska introduced a key change. He heard that dogs from Siberia were good racers in cold weather, so he ordered three teams of Siberian huskies for the third All Alaska Sweepstakes in 1910.

John "Iron Man" Johnson (above, far right) won the third All Alaska Sweepstakes mushing one of Ramsay's teams. No one has ever beat his time of 74 hours, 14 minutes, and 37 seconds.

Archives, University of Alaska Fairbanks

One Devoted Husky

Besides Ramsay, other racers used Siberian huskies in the early 1910s, including Leonhard Seppala. He and his dog Togo became a famous racing duo with a funny history. After Seppala sold Togo when the animal was a puppy, the new owners returned the dog because of his

Seppala and his dogs. Courtesy of Candy Waugaman

bad behavior. When Seppala sold him a second time, Togo escaped through the window and found his way back to Seppala's kennel. He followed Seppala's dog team 10 miles away, determined to join the pack. Seppala finally accepted him, and Togo eventually won races as the lead dog of the team.

"Togo"
Courtesy of Candy Waugaman

Seppala toured the states with his dogs, including Togo (above).

Racing soon started in other parts of the United States. In 1917, the American Dog Derby was the first all-American race (Alaska was only a US territory and not yet a state). It followed a 55-mile trail from West Yellowstone, Montana, to Ashton, Idaho. Tud Kent won the first race and five more after that.

The Great Race of Mercy

In 1925, Nome, Alaska, was hit with diphtheria, a disease that causes inflammation of the heart. Diphtheria can be fatal, and the only medicine, or serum, was more than 1,000 miles away in Anchorage. Alaska didn't have roads between cities, railroad tracks didn't travel that far west, and the weather was too blustery to fly airplanes. The only way to transport the medicine

A crowd in 1915 gathers for the start of the 8th All Alaska Sweepstakes in Nome. Courtesy of Candy Waugaman

was by sled dog. Twenty of the best sled dog teams in Alaska were asked to help. The medicine was transported to the city of Nenana by train and was then relayed from sled dog team to sled dog team over 600 miles. Bill Shannon and his nine dogs started the trip, but Seppala, Togo, and their team of dogs completed the longest stretch. They traveled 170 miles to the relay point and carried the medicine 91 miles to the next dog team. The last relay team (musher Gunnar Kaasen and

his lead dog Balto) raced the medicine to Nome in time to help those who were sick. The frantic five-day relay is known as the Great Race of Mercy, or the Serum Run.

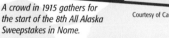

Map of Alaska.

To encourage sled dog racing as a worldwide sport, there was a three-day sled dog exhibition race at the 1928 Olympics. The sport returned to the Olympics as a demonstration in 1932 but hasn't been back since.

15

The Idea of the Iditarod

One of the most famous annual races, the Iditarod, started in 1967. Alaskans wanted to honor the sled dogs of the Serum

Sometimes mushers put coats on their sled dogs to keep them warm. Here is Rick Swenson and his team at the 2001 Iditarod Race.

© 2007 Jeff Schultz / AlaskaStock.com

Run, the Gold Rush, and the post office, and celebrate their state's 100th anniversary. Joe Redington Sr. and Dorothy Page raised prize money and cleared a small section of the original Gold Rush trail, the Iditarod. The Iditarod Trail Seppala Memorial Race was only 27 miles, from Knik to Big Lake. Today mushers and sled dogs race the length of the Serum Run – 1,150 miles from

In 1985, the Iditarod had its first female winner: Libby Riddles of Alaska (above). Here she is racing in Jackson Hole, Wyoming, in 1998. She had two lead dogs: Xerox (on the left) and Vinnie (on the right).

J. Bick

Anchorage to Nome. Teams of 12-16 dogs race for 10-17 days. Terry Adkins and Rick Swenson are true Iditarod veterans. They have both competed in 20 races.

The Chosen Ones

Sled dogs run best at dusk and dawn.

Not all dogs can be part of a sled dog team. They have to enjoy racing and get along with other dogs. They must be able to jump obstacles, such as branches on the trail. Unlike horse jockeys, mushers don't use reins. Dogs must be able to follow vocal sounds and commands. The dogs are connected to the sled by ganglines. Some ganglines have one lead dog at the head of the pack pulling the gang hitch. Two lead dogs working together form a double hitch. Dogs can be linked single file or in a fan shape.

Each spot on the gangline has a different role. The front dog (the lead dog) guides the team. The point dogs (swing dogs) run behind the lead and keep the sled on the trail during turns. Behind them, the team dogs help pull the sled. The wheel dogs run closest to the sled. If the sled gets caught, their job is to pull it loose.

Most sled dogs are born in the far north. Common breeds are the Alaskan malamute and the Siberian husky. Alaskan malamutes are the best dogs for heavy loads. They weigh between 75 and 85 pounds. The Siberian husky is bred for speed at only 35-60 pounds. The most popular breed of dog for the sport is the Alaskan husky, a Siberian husky / malamute cross that can carry heavy loads with great endurance.

16

Trivia Time

Not everyone races with huskies. In 1988, John Suter of Chugiak in Alaska ran some standard poodles in the Iditarod. Three of the dogs made it all the way and the team came in 38th out of 52.

Taking Care

In official sled dog races, dog and musher care is taken very seriously. Veterinarians examine all of the dogs before the race, checking their heart rate and looking for cuts and bruises. For long races, checkpoints are set up. The nearby townspeople cook food and bring supplies to these rest stops. Here, vets check the dogs again. Sometimes the checkpoint is a building; other times it's only a tent. Mushers can sleep indoors or bundle up outside with a sleeping bag. The dogs must sleep outside on straw beds so their temperature is regulated.

Mushing 101

Good mushers are just as important as strong teams of dogs. Mushers have to stand on the sled for hours in the cold and need to know when it's time to rest. If a musher gets tired and muddles his commands, the dogs may become confused. Mushers also need to be familiar with how far and fast each dog can run. Sometimes they need to massage their dogs' muscles if they cramp. Mushers know each dog intimately, by name, appearance, behavior, and personality. They are the pack leaders of the dog teams.

Learn the Lingo

- **Dogs in basket:** injured or tired dogs that ride to the next checkpoint on the sled
- **Dropped dogs:** dogs in basket are left in the care of the nearest checkpoint veterinarian
- **Mush:** to travel by dog sled; also used as a command
- **Musher:** the person who drives the dog sled
- **Scratching:** when a sick or injured musher drops out of a race
- **Trail:** what mushers call out to each other to get the right-of-way during a race

Dog Commands:
- **Hike:** "Get going"
- **Gee:** "Turn right"
- **Haw:** "Turn left"

Pet dogs eat about 800 calories a day. During a race, such as the lengthy and cold Iditarod, sled dogs require so much energy that they eat about 10,000 calories a day! They also need a chance to rest, like these Siberian huskies, above.

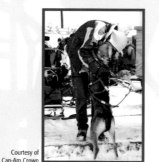

Courtesy of Can-Am Crown

Just like pet dogs, sled dogs need some TLC before and after a race. This photo is from the 2007 Can-Am Sled Dog Race.

Sometimes mushers protect their dogs' paws with booties. Throughout the race, the booties need to be changed as they wear out and adjusted if they slip. On very rough trails, the booties are sometimes replaced as often as every 10 miles. Here is Kathy Lesinski of Connecticut at the start of the 2007 Willard Jalbert Jr. Can-Am Crown, a 60-mile race in Maine.

Courtesy of Can-Am Crown

An Unstoppable Sport

Today sled dog races still take place in states such as Idaho, Maine, Minnesota, Montana, and Wisconsin. Mushers now wear thinner synthetic materials instead of animal skins, and they ride on fiberglass, plastic, or aluminum sleds. Sled dog racing is the official sport of Alaska, and the famous Iditarod race is held every year.

Ski the H₂O

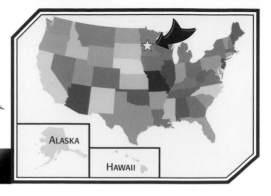

ALASKA

HAWAII

Skiing can be fun when there's snow on the ground, but what's a die-hard skier to do in the summer? Ralph Samuelson of Minnesota thought of a solution in 1922, when at the age of 18, he tried to create skis for water. Like most inventors, his first attempts weren't successful. He tried using staves (or sides) of a barrel and regular snow skis before finally creating his own skis out of pieces of wood. He shaped wood slabs and then boiled them so they would be flexible enough to curve. Then, he used a window sash attached to the boat as a cord to hold on to. He also found that he needed a good method to get himself

In addition to skiing behind a boat, Samuelson (above) sometimes skied behind a plane because it could reach higher speeds.   AWSEF Water Ski Museum/Hall of Fame

upright. Eventually he had the idea to lean back and keep the fronts of the skis out of the water. When it all came together, the sport of water skiing was born.

Sport Model   Safety Model   Speed Model

DOLPHIN AKWA-SKEES

Courtesy of the Huntington Historical Society

This ad for Akwa-Skees is from 1925.

Soon thereafter, many variations of water skiing were invented. In 1924, New Yorker Fred Waller, a special effects technician, created skis on which to mount a movie camera. In his design, the two water skis (instead of the skier) were attached to the boat by a rope and the skis also had a rope that the skier held on to. At first, the purpose of his skis was for movie making, but later Waller realized that these skis could be used for recreation. In 1925, he sold them under the name "Akwa-Skees."

Akwa-Skees had the rope attached to the skis. Notice Waller filming the women as he skis as well.   Courtesy of the Huntington Historical Society

Samuelson himself took the activity a step further in 1925 by becoming the first person to ski jump, using a diving platform greased with lard. He also was the first to speed ski, using a World War I flying boat that pulled him at a speed of 80 mph.

Photo from the 1949 World War Water Ski Championships. Jumpers would normally wear two skis, so this skier either lost a ski going up the ramp or was participating in the trick event.   AWSEF Water Ski Museum/Hall of Fame

USA Water Ski

AWSEF Water Ski Museum/Hall of Fame

This photo was taken at the first Water Ski National Championships in 1939. Slalom, shown here, used flags instead of buoys, and slalom skiers back then skied on two skis rather than one.

In 1939, Dan Hains, the first person to manufacture water skis, was asked to organize a water ski show for the World's Fair in New York. This inspired him to create the American Water Ski Association (which is now part of USA Water Ski). Hains created the three divisions of water skiing for competitions, which are still in place today: slalom, tricks, and jump.

At the first American Water Ski Association (AWSA) National Championships, held in Long Island, New York, the slalom course contained flags (instead of buoys as used today), but they were lined up in a straight row instead of staggered. Both the boat and the skier went around the flags! The tricks division featured skiers who removed one ski and held it over their head while they performed a stunt. The jump division had a platform made with wooden rollers, which helped to create less friction. The National Championships is now an annual competition that has taken place every year since 1939, except during World War II (1942-1945).

Barefoot'n

AWSEF Water Ski Museum/Hall of Fame

It's hard to track who the first person to ski barefoot was, but Pope (above) was one of the first to be photographed doing it.

In 1947, two Florida men, Dick Pope Jr. and A.G. Hancock, were credited separately as being the first to throw their water skis to the wind and attempt to water ski barefoot. The barefooted variation of the sport then debuted at water ski shows in Florida. It wasn't until 1961 that the American Barefoot Club began (the club later became a discipline of AWSA). To join, members were required to stay upright on the water for at least 60 seconds. Today, barefoot skiers participate in many of the same events as those who use skis. They perform tricks barefoot, including skiing backward and on one foot. They also do slalom skiing, but they ski around the wake of the water instead of around buoys. Barefoot skiers can even do jumps. Not using skis requires a faster boat speed and a lower jumping surface (around 18 inches versus 6 feet). Does this sound painful? Just imagine how some barefoot water skiers patch a bummed foot during a competition: with superglue.

Another Water Skier to Know

Jennifer Calleri-Schwenk (below) began water skiing in 1973 in Wisconsin when she was only four years old. By the time she was eight, she was able to climb a pyramid and performed in her first national show ski championship. At age 10 she learned how to ski barefoot by skiing between the skis of a fellow show skier. She was a skilled barefoot skier and went on to win many competitions, including the Willa Cook Swivel Ski Award at the 1986 Water Ski Show Nationals. She is currently the United States' most decorated female barefoot skier of all time. In 2002, she was inducted into the Water Ski Hall of Fame, at age 33.

AWSEF Water Ski Museum/Hall of Fame

Foiled!

Another spin-off of water skiing is hydrofoiling, invented in the early 1960s by Walter Woodward from Massachusetts. Hydrofoiling is based on the early designs of hydrofoil boats, which lift out of the water. In hydrofoiling, a rider sits on a chair attached to the board. Underneath the board is a long pole and a front and rear wing. Once the rider gets going, the board actually lifts above the water. Hydrofoiling is good for rougher water, since the skier is fully above – not touching – the water. Now there are variations on hydrofoiling, including using a surfboard and wind surfing (also called kitefoilboarding).

Buster MacCalla started skiing in the 1940s. Here he is in the 1960s on an early model hydrofoil (notice there is no seat on early hydrofoils).

AWSEF Water Ski Museum/Hall of Fame

AWSEF Water Ski Museum/Hall of Fame

Geno Yauchler of Florida, on a modern hydrofoil. The Hydrofoil Association named him Athlete of the Year in 2005 and 2006.

One Ski, Two Skis ... and Helmets?

Today, variations on water skiing continue. People now water ski on wakeboards and kneeboards. More advanced skiers use one ski, called a slalom ski, that they attach to one foot first and then place their other foot into once they are upright. Skis today are more custom designed for the different disciplines of skiing. Fins are placed on the bottom rear of the ski to help make sharp turns and to slow down. The sport of slalom uses a special single ski that has a deep fin with an attached "wing." Skis for jumping are longer and have fins on them. Trick skis do not have fins.

Speed skiing, or water ski racing, requires different equipment as well. The sport uses a single ski that is longer, and because the skiers are traveling so fast (almost 100 miles per hour), they wear helmets, wetsuits, and sometimes neck braces. Instead of holding on to the rope with their hands, they put it around their midsection (this is a special rope and should not be tried with a regular tow line). Water skiers now are not only towed by boats, but also by other motorized vehicles, such as Jet Skis.

Speed skiers like Erin Saunders (above) reach peeds around 100 mph.

AWSEF Water Ski Museum/Hall of Fame

Skurfers were early wakeboards, made in the 1980s. This one was signed by Tony Finn, a California surfer who created the first Skurfer.

AWSEF Water Ski Museum/Hall of Fame

Tournament Time

Water skiing is a popular sport today with over 1,000 tournaments each season sanctioned by USA Water Ski alone. It joined the Olympics as an exhibition sport in 1972 and remains in its "recognized sports" category. It also became part of the X Games in 1995, starting with barefoot jumping. The following year, wakeboarding joined the X Games.

Today, water skiing competitions are held for all ages, including adults 85 and over. Even kids nine years and under can compete in several events (not in speed skiing, however). It's never too early to set a record: at the age of eight, current World Slalom and Overall Champion Regina Jaquess started competing and set a record in slalom. She has gone on to win 40 slalom records.

Jaquess competing in slalom (above) and jumping (right) at the 2005 World Championships.

Photos by Jim Jaquess

Skiing Safely

Water skiing is a sport that requires proper safety measures to be followed at all times. Besides the driver, there needs to be at least one other person in the boat, called a spotter or observer. Communication is important between the skier, the driver, and the observer. By using a hand signal, the skier can motion whether to speed up, slow down, stop, or go back to the dock. The dangers of the activity include falling incorrectly and skiing too close to other boats, skiers, docks, and unseen obstacles in the water. Water skiers should always wear a life jacket.

Joe Ray, shown here water skiing, runs Adaptive Aquatics, a water ski school in Alabama for people with disabilities.

AWSEF Water Ski Museum/Hall of Fame

Learn the Lingo

➤ **Bunny hop:** a term used in wakeboarding when the skier jumps without the help of a wake

➤ **Rooster tail:** the high wave that boats, and some skis, create

➤ **Swivel skiing:** is a type of show skiing that uses a swivel binder on a single ski that allows the skier to rotate 360 degrees while the ski continues in a straight line

➤ **Wakeboard:** a short board that resembles a surfboard in shape, on which the skier stands with both feet

21

Bounce on a Trampoline

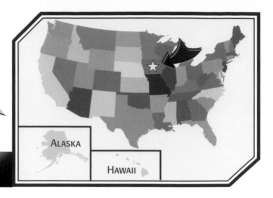

Bouncing Becomes Contagious

As a child in Iowa, George Nissen saw circus acrobats perform trapeze tricks and somersault safely onto the netting below. A bouncing surface that big had so many possibilities, especially for a boy with a background in gymnastics, tumbling, and diving. After graduating from high school, Nissen started to tinker and invent. He combined circus teeter boards and trapeze nets, searching for a way to perform diving tricks on land. First he built round trampolines for equal weight distribution, but the circular apparatus took up too much space. Next he tried rectangular trampolines, the shape of school gymnasiums. This way, more trampolines could fit into gyms.

Nissen (center, foreground) with the 1965 World Professional Trampoline Championships winners: Gary Erwin (far left), 1st place; George Hery, 2nd place; Ronnie Munn, 3rd place; and Johnny Hamilton, 4th place.

At the University of Iowa in the 1930s, his gymnastics coach was Larry Griswold, a champion tumbler and wrestler and a talented vaudeville clown. Griswold gathered talented students to tumble, tap dance, and teeter board in the Annual Iowa Circus. With help from the school wrestling coach, Mike Howard, Griswold and Nissen built a trampoline for the circus. They made the bed, or jumping area, out of tent canvas stretched over a junkyard metal frame. The design was a hit at the school circus. Once the summer of 1936 arrived, it was time to have others try out this new invention.

Griswold (above) became one of the top entertainers in the 1950s. His comedy act, which was shown on TV and on stages around the world, featured a trampoline, as seen here on the right. He would make a trampoline look like a pool and then jump on it from a diving board.

Putting the Y in Jumpy and the Jump in the Y

Twenty-two-year-old Nissen brought this "magic carpet" to the local YMCA camp where he worked, and all of the kids loved it. He redesigned the heavy frame into a portable, collapsible model better designed for touring. After graduating from college, Nissen and his friends tumbled and clowned throughout the United States and Mexico. While in Mexico City, they stayed at the YMCA where Nissen got talked into joining the diving team. He thought the Spanish word for diving board, *el trampolin*, would make a great name for his magic carpets, so he trademarked the invention under the name "Trampoline."

Now that Nissen had a name and a product, he was ready to try to sell it. When sports equipment stores turned him down, he brought the trampoline into schools and put on a tumbling and trampoline act for the students. After every performance, Nissen invited students to try the apparatus themselves. They had so much fun that schools began to buy trampolines for their gymnasiums. Nissen sold them for $150 each, assembly required.

Timing is Everything

During World War II, physical education teachers and coaches (Nissen's biggest customers) were drafted to serve in the war. This could have been the end of the trampoline, but Nissen found a new market. In 1942, he and Griswold created the Griswold-Nissen Trampoline and Tumbling Company to market trampolines to the military. Nissen went to military camps, where cadets – especially pilots and parachutists – could use the trampoline in their training and physical fitness programs. Trampoline use took off.

These photos show trampolines being used by the military for training during World War II. The photo above is of Newt Loken, first lieutenant in charge of fitness activities, demonstrating a somersault on the flight deck of the USS Prince William in the early 1940s. The photo on the left shows Loken performing a back somersault in a layout position while Navy academy students watch.

Nissen enlisted in the Navy and continued to sell trampolines to the military. Although he had a strong market for his product, he continued to look for other customers. Other trampoline enthusiasts started building recreational trampoline knock-offs like the Acromat and the Tumble-teen. Nissen's hard work paid off, and trampolining became a sport. With standardized equipment and coach supervision, the first official "rebound tumbling" competition took place in Texas in 1946.

In the 1950s and 1960s, trampolines were used in public physical education programs (middle school through college). In the above photo, high school students are using Nissen trampolines at a California school.

Jumping Forward

Although Nissen sometimes gets sole credit for the modern trampoline, Larry Griswold was a co-creator. The two built the apparatus, performed shows as a team, and started the first trampoline manufacturing company. In the 1940s, Griswold wrote *Trampoline Tumbling*, which Nissen contributed to. The book explained how to perform simple and complex trampoline exercises. While Griswold was more interested in the book, Nissen cared more about the invention itself. By the time the book was published in 1948, the two men had gone their separate ways.

Nissen continued selling trampolines and started to have success overseas. People in England, the former Soviet Union, Japan, South Africa, and parts of South America bought into the bouncing craze, and trampolining went global. The Nissen Trampoline Corporation had a headquarters in Iowa and opened a second one in Switzerland. This is where the first international trampolining competition, the Nissen Cup, began in 1958 and still takes place today.

Before there were weightlessness chambers, astronauts would practice various body positions on trampolines in order to prepare for the feeling of weightlessness in space flight. Here is a trampoline performance in the 1960s at the Houston Space Center. Notice the astronauts in the background.

Photos from the collection of Lani Loken

Trivia Time

In the 1960s, Nissen got a little sales help from a kangaroo. He rented a kangaroo from a Long Island animal supplier that had two of the animals for rent: one for $50 and one for $150. Nissen splurged $150 for the animal that didn't kick as hard and trained it to jump on one end of a trampoline while he jumped on the other end. A steady supply of apricots kept the kangaroo cooperative. Photos were taken for Nissen Trampoline advertisements.

By 1959, "jump centers" opened in the United States. For a quarter or two, people could play and gymnasts could train on trampolines. Nissen worried about amateur accidents on unsupervised trampolines. Most jump centers were understaffed and uncertified despite his best efforts to regulate the purchase and use of trampolines. People were getting hurt, so some centers closed.

Nissen on his trampoline with a kangaroo.

Courtesy of George Nissen

An instructional Spaceball booklet from the 1960s (right). Nissen invented the game of Spaceball, a version of which is still enjoyed at game centers today. It's played on a trampoline with a ball, a net, and elastic backstops behind the players for safety.

Courtesy of George Nissen

As jumping centers were shutting down, competitions on official Nissen trampolines continued. In 1964, the first World Trampoline Championships took place in England. Dan Millman from California won the men's division. Judy Wills Cline from Mississippi won the women's title and later made it into the *Guinness Book of World Records* for the most trampoline world titles (10). In 1966, the NCAA (the National Collegiate Athletic Association) started the Nissen Award for the most outstanding gymnast of the year.

Judy Wills Cline (in the middle) was the first woman to win the World Trampoline Championships.

From the collection of Judy Wills Cline

US trampolining could have made a breakthrough in 1980 as it was supposed to be an exhibition sport in the Moscow Olympic Games. However, the United States and other countries boycotted the games over the Soviet invasion of Afghanistan. Instead of being a featured sport, trampolining was only part of the opening ceremony entertainment, and the performance was not televised in the United States. Trampolining would have to wait to be shared as a sport with the general public.

★ "I was the first

trampolinist to perform a twisting triple somersault (I did this when I was 14) and to win a world championship at 18 years of age."

– Dan Millman –

Millman in 1985 doing an Arabian dive, which is also called a half-twisting dive.

M. Nelson

In 1969, Judith Ford, Miss Illinois, proved that trampolining can be an award-winning talent. Ford was an elite trampolinist who performed a competitive trampoline routine for the talent segment of the Miss America contest. She won the title of Miss America that year.

Courtesy of Judith Ford

Bouncing Up and On

Paul Parilla

Jennifer Parilla from California was the first American to take part in the trampoline event at the 2000 Olympic Games in Sydney, Australia. She was the only American to compete that year and in 2004 at the Olympics in Athens, Greece.

Steve Lange

In 2000, trampolining was recognized outside the gymnastics community. It finally became an official sport at the Sydney Olympic Games.

In the time it takes to read this paragraph, an entire trampoline routine could be performed. Most individual routines are made up of 10 tricks, 20 to 25 feet in the air, done within about 20 seconds. This isn't the only trampoline event. In synchronized trampolining, two athletes bounce on separate trampolines side by side and perform identical routines at the same time.

Synchronized trampolining at the USA Trampoline & Tumbling National Championships held in Nashville, Tennessee, in June 2004.

Courtesy of Paul Parilla

Athletes have also used trampolines to cross train for other sports. Cheerleaders master their tricks on a trampoline, as do extreme sports athletes. BMXers, snowboarders, skateboarders, and wakeboarders also practice their moves (with or without their equipment) on trampolines.

Watch Where You Jump

Competitive and backyard trampolines are very different, but both require crucial safety precautions. Competitive trampolining requires spotters to assist the jumper if needed. Backyard trampolines are often enclosed to help keep the jumper from falling off. With all trampolines, only one person should jump at a time and should bounce in the center of the bed. The International Trampoline Industry Association (ITIA), created in 1999 and headed by Lani Loken, a professional trampolinist herself, promotes trampoline use in sport, recreation, and fitness, and encourages public awareness of safe trampoline use.

A pike jump.

The trampoline is now a common piece of gymnastics equipment. Nissen worked hard to spread the word and was successful. Today, his name for the apparatus – trampoline – continues on.

Learn the Lingo

➤ **Bed:** the bouncing, or rebounding, surface of the trampoline

➤ **Front drop:** to drop from a standing position to the stomach with the hands under the chin and legs tucked underneath the body

➤ **Pike jump:** to jump with the legs together in front and touch the toes with the hands

➤ **Seat drop:** to contact the trampoline bed with the seat, legs, and hands

➤ **Spotter:** the person who stands at the edge of the trampoline to protect or assist the performer doing a stunt or routine

➤ **Straddle jump:** to jump with the legs out to both sides and touch the toes with the hands

➤ **Swivel hips:** to perform a half twist and fall to a seat drop

Jam with Flying Discs

It All Began with Popcorn

Morrison surrounded by Frisbees.

Wham-O

W ho would have thought that a can of popcorn could be inspiration for a game with worldwide appeal? In California in 1937, Fred Morrison discovered that the lids to large popcorn tins, which were popular at the time, were fun to fling around. He found that metal cake pans worked too, and were easier to come by. A couple of years after his initial discovery, he sold metal cake pans, on the beaches of California, to throw through the air. He redesigned the cake pan, using plastic injection molding, which made it fly better than metal. This was the first plastic flying disc, which Morrison and his business partner, Warren Franscioni, sold in 1948 as the Pipco Flyin-Saucer. It was named the "Flyin-Saucer" because of the scare of UFOs (Unidentified Flying Objects, also called "flying saucers") that was all over the news at that time. (Pipco produced the discs.)

'Flying Saucers' Cover Continent; No Proven Cause to Solve Mystery

UFOs in the news. *Montreal Gazette*, July 7, 1947

Phil Kennedy Collection

These cake pans were sold as flying discs by Morrison and his wife, Lu, for 25 cents each.

I n 1955, Morrison created a new disc called the "Pluto Platter." It became so popular that Wham-O bought it from him. According to popular legend, Rich Knerr, co-owner of Wham-O, renamed the toy "Frisbee" after the Frisbie Baking Company whose famous pie plates were always flung around by college kids. Knerr supposedly misspelled "Frisbie" as "Frisbee" when he trademarked the name. The Frisbee debuted in 1957 and came in red, yellow, blue, green, and white. The word *Frisbee* is often misused for any flying disc. It is actually the brand name that was given to the original Wham-O flying disc.

1957 Pluto Platter

1957 Pluto Platter

2007 50th Anniversary Gold Pro-Frisbee

Wham-O

1958 Frisbee

1965 Pro-Frisbee

An original Pipco Flyin-Saucer, like this one, could be worth over $1,000 today.

Phil Kennedy Collection

26

Joel Silver (in black, far left) brought disc flying to his high school. Pictured here is the original Columbia High School Varsity Frisbee Squad (1969).

Mark Epstein

In 1969, Columbia High School students in New Jersey wanted to take flying disc games up a notch. They saw a way to make flying discs more of a sport than a recreational activity and invented "Ultimate Frisbee." It's now referred to as just "Ultimate." In this game, points are scored as the disc is passed over a goal line. If it is dropped, the disc goes to the other team. There are no referees for Ultimate – the players keep track of their own points and fouls. More than 40 different countries now play.

Irv Kalb of Rutgers out-jumps a Princeton player in the first intercollegiate Ultimate Frisbee game (1972).

Irv Kalb

Besides Ultimate, there are many other flying disc-related sports. "Guts" is a game of catch in which a team tries to throw the disc to the other team, making the disc difficult for them to grasp. "Disc golf" is a sport that has had success around the world. Standardized in 1976 by Ed Headrick, players of the game have designated tee-off areas and "holes," which instead of being holes in the ground, are targets to hit, such as trees and telephone poles or baskets for the disc to land in.

Hikari Hayato of Japan tipping the disc at the 2001 World Games.

Larry Imperiale
ColoradoPowder.com

In disc golf, players aim for a target – in this case, up in the air. In the United States alone, there are almost 1,000 disc golf courses.

Another popular activity is "freestyle," which combines art and athleticism. Improvised routines are mostly done in pairs or threes and are performed to high-energy music. Freestylers do stunts while keeping a flying disc in motion, like air brushing or tipping (see Learn the Lingo, p. 28), or by catching it along the rim. A key component of freestyling is a delay. One type is called a nail delay, which is spinning the disc in its center while balancing it on a fingernail. Some players – male and female – wear a fake nail to protect their real nail.

There are various organizations for the different flying disc activities. Most offer competitions around the United States, and even worldwide.

Aerobies are flying rings. In 2003, an Aerobie Pro Ring was used to break the Guinness World Record for the longest throw using an object (without a velocity-aiding feature). The ring traveled 1,333 feet.

Aerobie, Inc.

So Many Discs, So Little Time

Today, there are hundreds of types of flying discs made for different uses. The reason for so many varieties is that the diameter and weight make a difference in how the discs fly. The classic disc for recreational use is about 90 grams. Discs used for playing Ultimate are larger in diameter and weigh about 175 grams. Freestyle discs are also larger but weigh slightly less, about 160 grams. Many freestylers prefer a slower disc so that they have time to do tricks. Disc golfers use different discs depending on whether players are teeing off, driving, or putting. The discs for long-range flight are more streamlined than discs for putting, which are blunter and give players more control.

Murphy at the World Beach Championships (1990).

Bill Bergner

The basic grip for throwing a flying disc.

"I was the first

person in my sport to include acrobatics. While most players were doing tricks with the flying disc by moving it around their bodies, I created a new style that involved moving my body around the disc. I was doing front and back somersaults, handstands, high-flying upside-down catches, and even front flips with it."

– Dave Murphy –

Learn the Lingo

➤ **Air brushing:** to keep a disc spinning by hitting it on the rim with a hand or foot

➤ **Hammer:** an overhead throw in which the disc flies upside down in the air

➤ **Hyzer:** angling the disc so that the side of the disc away from the throwing hand is lower

➤ **Jam:** playing freestyle

➤ **Scarecrow:** catching a flying disc at head level without being able to see it (arms are out from the body in a "T" position, like a scarecrow)

➤ **Taco:** when the disc gets bent in half and curls up

➤ **Tipping:** hitting a spinning disc in the center, usually with a finger, and causing it to bounce up

➤ **Toe jam:** using a toenail instead of a fingernail to delay or spin the disc

➤ **UD crow:** a scarecrow catch with the disc upside down (UD)

Trivia Time

The World Flying Disc Federation keeps track of records set with flying discs in categories such as distance; Throw, Run, Catch (where a person throws the disc and runs to catch it with one hand); and maximum time aloft (the time a disc is kept suspended in the air). The original record for keeping a flying disc in the air was 16.72 seconds, set by Don Cain in 1984 in Pennsylvania.

Disc Dogs

Flying discs aren't popular only with humans. Dogs have their own flying disc competitions as well. The first recorded all-dog meet was held in 1974 at California State University, where an Australian sheepdog named Hyper Hank was the crowned champion.

In the 1970s, Irv Lander and Alex Stein raised the status of disc dog events, creating canine world championships that still exist today. In 1975, Stein's dog, Ashley Whippet, was the first winner of this competition, and was victorious for three years straight. Disc dogs, as they are called, can compete in such categories as distance, accuracy, freestyle, and pairs freestyle, which has two humans and one dog. Any breed of dog can compete – even small dogs, who now have their own category called "microdog class."

Ashley Whippet with Irv Lander and Ashley's owner Alex Stein (in the baseball hat).

Photos courtesy of The Ashley Whippet Museum

Dogs use a special disc. It's usually smaller than a regular disc and more durable, because dogs' sharp teeth can pierce it. Discs for larger dogs are about 130 grams and 8.75 inches in diameter, and discs for smaller dogs are about 90 grams and 7 inches in diameter. The discs can be made from shatterproof material for play in extremely cold areas, or from a special plastic for dogs with sensitive mouths. Discs can even be coated with glow-in-the-dark paint for night practices.

Dog owners need to be sure to allow a doggie bathroom break before the competition begins. If the dog decides to go during its turn, the clock keeps ticking.

Another Flying Disc Thrower to Know

Larry Imperiale of Colorado performed the highest-altitude freestyle move by jamming on a mountain summit in Nepal – more than 20,000 feet above sea level. He has also gone into the Dead Sea, the lowest place on earth – more than 1,312 feet below sea level – and has jammed there. Imperiale is talented at sea level as well. He has the most Major Open wins of any flying disc freestyle competitor: 18. He not only competes in Ultimate and freestyle, he is also well-versed in "overall," which includes disc golf, distance, and accuracy.

Larry Imperiale performs a chest roll on top of a Himalayan mountain.

Larry Imperiale ColoradoPowder.com

Jump on a Skateboard

Sidewalk Surfing

The skateboard's roots go back to the early 1900s, when scooter-boards were made across the United States from an apple crate or dresser drawer, a piece of wood, and an old roller skate. In the late 1950s, "sidewalk surfing" emerged when the scooter's crate was removed.

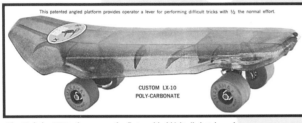

This patented angled platform provides operator a lever for performing difficult tricks with ½ the normal effort.

CUSTOM LX-10 POLY-CARBONATE

The Makaha LX10, above, was the first molded kicktail skateboard.

The shorter Makaha skateboards were better for turning, and the longer boards were better for speed. These boards are from 1963.

Surfer Mike Purpus, left, rides a board with a prototype kicktail (the turned-up end of a skateboard). Stevenson is the inventor of the kicktail.

It took someone in the world of surfing to design a better skateboard. In 1963, Larry Stevenson, a body surfer and a West Coast publisher of a surf magazine, *Surf Guide*, created a professional skateboard based on the shape of a surfboard. Some surfers felt that balancing on a skateboard was similar to surfing and would be good practice for when they couldn't be out on the water. Stevenson started a company called Makaha, which held the first skateboard contest in 1963 in California. Skaters were judged on tricks such as handstands and high jumps. Makaha also sponsored the first official skateboard team, which included Woody Woodward and Brad "Squeak" Blank.

Skateboarders quickly learned that riding on the pavement was not a smooth experience. Roller-skate wheels were made of clay, which meant that they locked up when the skaters hit a bump on the pavement. This caused riders to wipe out. During the mid 1960s, skateboarding was considered to be dangerous and was even outlawed in some cities.

Early skateboards, like this 1963 Makaha Commander, were shaped like surfboards.

Photos courtesy of Makaha, LLC

Reinventing the Wheel

In the early 1970s, surfer Frank Nasworthy from Virginia started manufacturing skateboard wheels out of urethane, a type of plastic. This material had great grip and easily rolled over small bumps. It allowed skaters to stay upright longer and perform more complicated maneuvers. This was a major turning point. Skaters everywhere, including the Zephyr Team, also called the Z-Boys, were eager to try the new wheels.

Courtesy of Craig B. Snyder

Some 1970s bubble gum trading cards, like the one seen here, featured skateboarding moves.

The Z-Boys were surfers-turned-skateboarders who lived in a section of Los Angeles referred to as Dogtown. The 12 teens, including Tony Alva and Stacy Peralta, helped shape the art and sport of skateboarding in the early 1970s. The Z-Boys tried to imitate famous surfers of the day on their new wheels. When they first entered the 1975 Skateboard Championships in Del Mar, California, their moves and tricks were completely different from anything the judges had ever seen. Their style was based on surfing, while others in the contest were performing tricks such as handstands and wheelies. Most of the Z-Boys ended up not placing, since no one knew how to score them. But from there, many of the Z-Boys went on to win other competitions or start their own skateboard companies – ever hear of Alva Skates or Powell Peralta Skateboards?

Learn the Lingo

- **360:** to spin the board on the back wheels all the way around

- **720:** two consecutive 360s

- **Coffin:** lying down on your back on the skateboard and putting your hands together on your chest

- **Goofy:** skating with the right foot in front instead of the left

- **Grind:** to slide on the edge of a surface, balancing on the area of the board between the wheels

- **Kick-turn:** to turn on the back wheels with the front wheels off the ground

- **Manual or wheelie:** riding the skateboard across a surface with the front wheels in the air

- **Vert:** a discipline of skateboarding that uses a vertical or sloped surface, such as a ramp

The skateboarding style of the Z-Boys resembled surfing. Alva is pictured here in the late 1970s skating in an empty pool.

CP/Everett Collection

Another Skateboarder to Know

Peggy Oki was one of the original members of the Z-Boys. At her first competition (the 1975 Skateboard Championships), she was told by other female contestants that it wasn't fair for her to skate in the girls' division because she skated more like a boy. The girls knew that Oki would be tough to beat. She ended up placing first in Women's Freestyle.

One of the Z-Boys asked Oki (left) to join their team after seeing her skate.

Jim Mahoney

Catch the ... *Cement* Wave?

Skateboarders were soon seen everywhere – even in empty swimming pools. Swimming-pool skating was first attempted in the 1960s, but it didn't catch on. Then, in 1976, a drought hit Southern California, and skateboarders were stoked. Because water was so precious, it couldn't be wasted on filling swimming pools. Skaters found that the smooth fishbowl shape of an empty pool was perfect for new tricks.

Later in 1976, the ultimate happened: the first concrete skate park opened in Port Orange, Florida. As they did in the pools, skaters rode up the banked concrete walls and performed tricks. A skate park was where Alan "Ollie" Gelfand did the first off-the-ground trick, or aerial. In 1977, this Floridian skater launched his famous move in which he popped his skateboard – while on it – into the air,

Craig B. Snyder

Gelfand, seen here in Florida in 1979, performs his signature move on the Hollywood Ramp, which he and his friends designed in 1978.

without using his hands. His friends started to refer to the move using Gelfand's nickname: Ollie. The name for the move stuck, and skateboarders everywhere started doing ollies. Soon thereafter, skaters discovered another aerial move: the frontside air, which entailed grabbing the board with one hand and bringing it into the air over the lip of the bowl (the edge of the skate park or pool) and landing back on the wall. Tony Alva is one of the first to be phtographed in the late 1970s doing a frontside air in a pool.

Bill Procko

Skate parks made it possible for skaters to practice their moves. Seen here is Cleo Coney in 1981 at the Sensation Basin skate park in Florida, which is also where Rodney Mullen practiced.

Kick-flippin' It Up a Notch

Through the 1970s, different forms of skateboarding took shape. Some skaters raced between cones for speed and accuracy, called "slalom." They also began to race downhill on longboards. Others liked doing tricks on flatland, which became known as "freestyle" skateboarding.

In addition to the ollie, the kick-flip is a basic freestyle move in skating today. A kick-flip, first done in 1975 by Curt Lindgren from California, is a move in which the skateboard is flipped 360 degrees while the skater is airborne, and then the skater lands back on the skateboard. In the 1980s, the ollie and a variation of the kick-flip were combined by Rodney Mullen to create new tricks that are used in street skating, such as heel-flips and 360 flips.

SkateBoarder
A SURFER PUBLICATION   VOL. 5, NO. 4 NOVEMBER 1978 $1.50

GETTING DOWN ON THE PIGS
A revolution in skateboards

EUROPEAN SKATE EXPOSÉ
'Don't give up on us yet!'
ROLLER RAGING
The rollerskate resurgence
QUIVERS – PART I

Courtesy of Dan Murray

In 1978, Gelfand and Mike Folmer were photographed for skate magazines. Although Gelfand was the inventor of the move, Folmer was the first person to be featured on the cover of a magazine doing an ollie (seen here).

Vert ramps for skateboarding were created from plywood that was curved into a U shape.

The deck of a skateboard is covered with a material called grip tape, which helps keep skaters' feet from slipping.

While some skaters liked freestyling, others preferred riding sloped surfaces and walls; this was called bank riding. Since most skate parks had closed in the 1980s because the insurance was too pricey, skaters began to build vertical ramps out of wood. This new form of skateboarding later became known as "vert" skateboarding. Early vert ramps were called half-pipes because of their shape. Skaters would perform tricks at both ends of the ramp.

One of the most well-known vert skateboarders, Tony Hawk, made a name for himself in the 1980s. At the age of 14, the practice paid off: Hawk went pro. He is credited with creating more than 80 skateboard moves – some variations and combinations of moves already invented, such as a finger flip backside air and a frontside stale fish 540.

Today, just about any surface is used for skateboarding. Even handrails and stairs offer new challenges to more advanced skaters. This is referred to as "street."

CP/Calgary Sun/Jim Wells

Hawk, seen here performing a jump during a 2001 demonstration, got his start in California skate parks.

But not everyone can perform such extreme skateboarding moves. There are many maneuvers that professionals attempt that should not be copied by a beginner or intermediate skater. Even pros wear helmets, as well as elbow and knee pads to avoid getting injured if they fall.

Skateboards have three main parts: the deck, the wheels, and the truck (the piece of metal the wheels are attached to).

Although skateboarding is still a young sport, it has come a long way. Clothing lines and shoes designed for skateboarders are worn by many. Video games have made skateboarding from the couch possible. Television viewers around the United States were finally able to watch the sport when it joined the X Games lineup in 1995. Even Tony Hawk, who had retired from skating, competed. Next stop for skateboarding: world recognition at the Olympics.

Todd Huber, skatelab.com

"The Tunnel of Love" (above) at the Skatelab Skateboarding Museum in California is made up of 2,000 skateboards, all from different decades.

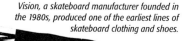

Vision, a skateboard manufacturer founded in the 1980s, produced one of the earliest lines of skateboard clothing and shoes.

Cruise with BMX

The Birth of BMX

Did you know that many of the masterminds behind bicycle motocross (BMX) were teenagers? It all started when they began riding the Schwinn Sting-Ray. Unlike other bikes in the 1960s, the Sting-Ray had smaller wheels, which made performing wheelies easier. It was also shaped more like a motorcycle, which sparked young riders' imaginations: if it looked like a motorcycle, it might ride like one too. Since many of the kids' dads were into motorcycle racing, the kids began racing their Sting-Rays in the pit area of the track. To look even more official, they added number plates to the fronts of their bikes.

R.L. Osborn (right) started in BMX racing and then joined Bob Haro in the world of freestyle. R.L.'s father, Bob Osborn (a.k.a. Oz), was also part of BMX, as a photographer and publisher of Bicycle Motocross Action magazine.

Breithaupt, seen here on an early BMX bike, helped make BMX a popular sport.

Who is often thought of as one of the founders of BMX? A 13-year-old. In 1970, Scot Breithaupt from California made Sting-Ray racing popular for kids on the West Coast. He held one of the first unofficial competitions in Long Beach, California, using a dirt field as the race course. His events attracted so many racers that he needed to get a lease for the land he was using. The land owner gave him a lease for a dollar a year. Breithaupt slapped five dollars on the table and was set for five years. He then began what he called the Bicycle United Motocross Society, known as B.U.M.S.

The 1971 motorcycle movie *On Any Sunday* brought to the rest of the United States what Breithaupt made popular on the West Coast. In an opening scene of the film, kids race their bikes like motorcycles. This opened the eyes of viewers across the nation to what would become bicycle motocross, named after the sport's similarities to all-terrain-motorcycle races, or motocross. Kids everywhere soon wanted to have number plates on the fronts of their bikes and become part of the sport.

In sidehack racing, the main rider was called the driver; the extra rider was called the monkey.

Photos from the film *Joe Kid on a Sting-Ray – The History of BMX*; www.JoeKidOnaStingray.com

In addition to competing on flatland, kids started to race down hills, and their bikes became airborne. When bike frames started cracking in two, riders quickly realized that the Sting-Ray was not designed for such hard wear and tear. Kids and their dads tried welding their bikes back together, and in some cases, they ended up changing the original design of the frame. In 1972, Rick Twomey, from California, fixed the problem by designing a bike with a better frame for racing. He also formed his own team called Rick's Bike Shop, which had some of the best racers of that time, including teens Thom Lund, John Palfreyman Jr., and Doug Takahashi. Because their team was so good, bike companies, such as Mongoose and Webco, sent them prototypes of bikes to try.

BMX racing started off small. Shown above is a 1970s race. Notice Bobby Encinas in the foreground wearing the Rick's Bike Shop jersey.

Photo from the film *Joe Kid on a Sting-Ray – The History of BMX;* www.JoeKidOnaStingray.com

Bicycle motocross had a strong following in California, but it needed a national organization to set standard rules for racing and safety. In 1972, Ernie Alexander, who ran mini-bike and motorcycle races in Indian Dunes, California, formed The National Bicycle Association (NBA), the first association for BMX riders. This helped other areas of the United States learn about the growing sport. From there, magazines and newspapers helped spread the word. One of the first publications to do so was *Bicycle Motocross News*. It was the first newspaper dedicated solely to the sport of BMX, and is also thought to be the first to use the term "BMX."

Bicycle Motocross Action was one of the first magazines for BMX. The debut issue was Dec. 1976/Jan. 1977.

Photo from the film *Joe Kid on a Sting-Ray – The History of BMX;* www.JoeKidOnaStingray.com

Trivia Time

You might have seen motorcycles that have a sidecar for a passenger (or for a dog). In the 1970s, BMX bikes had the same feature! In what was called "sidehack racing," a sidecar would be attached to the bike and a second rider would help navigate the bike to jump hills and do just about everything that was done with single-rider bikes.

Magazines did more than just inspire kids everywhere to ride. As BMX athletes posed for magazine photos, they would try out new moves, like lifting an arm and leg off the bike while in the air. This created a new direction in BMX: freestyle.

The Art of BMX

Haro (seen here doing a one-handed, one-footed kick-turn in the late 1970s) helped pioneer freestyling.

James Cassimus

In the late 1970s, 18-year-old Bob Haro tried out tricks never done before, such as the rock walk (riding in a circle and hitting the brakes so the bike turns in a half-circle on the front wheel, and then goes back the other way on the back wheel). He found that his bike was not made for what he wanted to do, so he designed his own bike: a freestyle bike that was lighter weight and better for trick-riding. Haro now has his own company, Haro Bikes, and is considered one of the pioneers of freestyle.

As other freestylers developed their signature moves, they also saw parts of the bike that needed improvement: if handlebars could spin 360 degrees, the rider wouldn't need to spin them back the way they started; with pegs on the wheels, riders could do tricks while standing or hopping on them. These new additions planted the seed for trick teams to form and travel around the United States in the early 1980s, sometimes performing during halftime at BMX races. Some of the moves freestyle riders like Eddie Fiola and Pat Romano did resembled circus acrobatics, such as riding while doing a handstand. Fiola and Romano were even stunt doubles for movies that featured tricks or stunts on bikes – check out *Rad* and *Jurassic Park* to see them in action.

Learn the Lingo

➤ **Brain bucket:** helmet

➤ **Bunny hop:** lifting the bike off both wheels

➤ **Dead sailor:** when the rider jumps but doesn't catch much height

➤ **Grind:** to slide on the bike's pegs along a ledge or rail

➤ **Huck:** to mess up a big trick

➤ **Park:** concrete areas with various dips and curved surfaces to do tricks on

➤ **Ramp up the jawn:** to tell someone to "jump the ramp"

John Palfreyman Jr. (J.P.), seen here in the mid 1970s, was one of the first BMXers to begin pool riding.

Photo from the film *Joe Kid on a Sting-Ray – The History of BMX*; www.JoeKidOnaStingray.com

While some freestyle bikers were practicing their tricks, others followed skateboarders into empty pools and rode on the smooth walls (see p. 32 of the skate-boarding section). Eventually, ramps called half-pipes were made out of curved pieces of plywood, and this gave birth to vert freestyling in the 1980s. Riders would pedal like crazy and then swoop into the air at the top of the vertical wall. There they would perform tricks, such as flips and 360s.

Hitting the Streets

In 1988, freestyling began to die out and street riding caught on. It quickly became popular because it uses a flat surface and can be done just about anywhere. Bikers could jump up or off stairs and grind on curbs and railings. Urban kids whose neighborhoods weren't set up for BMX racing or vert could street ride easily.

In 1995, BMX joined the X Games and gained world recognition. New sports heroes were born – Mat Hoffman from Oklahoma placed first in vert, and Jay Miron of British Columbia placed first in park and third in vert. The X Games now has divisions in freestyle vert, vert best trick, park, and dirt.

BMX is still very hot today, and BMX racing will soon become an Olympic event. The names of legends live on as BMX greats create their own companies and teams, including Haro, Hoffman, and Dave Mirra (who has won 14 gold medals at the X Games).

Today there are over 11,000 organized BMX racing events a year in the United States.

Hoffman doing a trick called "peacock" at Woodward Camp in Pennsylvania.

Hoffman Enterprises
Photo by Michael Castillo

Sportin' a Brain Bucket

Safety equipment is important for all BMX disciplines. This can prevent serious injury caused by crashing or falling. Many competitions require riders to wear a helmet, long pants that are tight fitting at the ankles (to avoid getting caught in the chain), long sleeves, knee, hip, and elbow pads, and a mouth guard. Not only do amateur BMX riders wear safety gear, but professionals are required to do the same. If you've ever watched riders like Mat Hoffman fly 20 feet in the air, you understand why!

Roger Snider

Surprisingly, Coffey, seen here on a vert wall, is afraid of heights!

Another BMX Pro to Know

Cory Coffey, a skateboarder turned BMX pro, was the first woman in the world to do a back flip on a bicycle. She now rides both ramp and dirt, and performs tricks such as no-handers and back flips.

Get in Snowboard Mode

ALASKA

HAWAII

Snurfin' Safari

It's the fastest-growing sport in the United States. Maybe you know it better as snowboarding, but for years it was called "Snurfing." It began in Michigan in 1965 when Sherman Poppen's young daughter, Wendy, wanted to surf during a snowstorm. Sherman took his daughter's wish as a challenge. He attached two skis side by side and added a rope to hold on to. His wife combined the words "snow" and "surf" and called the invention the "Snurfer." The Snurfer was an instant hit. Six months later, Poppen sold his idea to Brunswick Sporting Goods. Many people considered the Snurfer a fun toy or a novelty, rather than the beginning of a true sport.

Snurfer ads from the 1960s. The Snurfer name belongs to Poppen. Had he not copyrighted the name, the sport of snowboarding might still be called Snurfing today.

Wintersticks

In 1970, East Coast surfer Dimitrije Milovich tried a new design for surfing on snow, based on the plastic cafeteria trays he watched college kids slide down hills on. The board, which he called the "Winterstick," was shorter than a surfboard and longer than a Snurfer. His business, Winterstick, was one of the first snowboard companies.

Other board designers in the 1970s included Bob Webber, Chuck Barfoot, and Tom Sims. They tried different materials, such as polyethylene and fiberglass, and experimented with adding fins (which they took off). Because Poppen owned the rights to the name Snurfer, all other boards were referred to as snowboards and still are today.

Wintersticks were made in two designs: the swallowtail (left, from 1978) and the roundtail (right, from 1986). The swallowtail was designed so that the tail end would sink and the front end would tilt out of the snow. It worked better in powder, while the roundtail was better for packed snow.

Marty Bodell

© 2007 Burton Snowboards

Bindings are now used to attach the boots to the board. Snowboards without bindings, like this 1981 snowboard (above), often had some sort of traction on the top of the board so that the rider wouldn't slip off. Some riders preferred boards without bindings because they could then switch their position as surfers do.

Burton Boards

Another Snurfer enthusiast also had ideas for the sport. Jake Burton worked on improving the snowboard, and by 1977, he had invented a flexible wood design with fins and foot traps made from water ski bindings. But his "Burton Board," as he called it, didn't catch on right away. One reason was the cost. Another problem was that Snurfer riders were still set on using only true Snurfer boards.

Burton began designing boards in 8th grade shop class. Here he is as an adult in the early 1980s shaping a snowboard.

Some snowboards, such as this 1987 Burton Cruzer, have a stomp pad (see p. 40) behind the front foot.

When Burton tried to enter a Michigan Snurfing competition in 1979 with his Burton Board, no one liked his new board. But when he showed just what the board could do (the foot traps made many new moves possible), people finally took notice of his new design. Later, when sales started coming in, he turned his house into a makeshift factory and filled orders from around the United States at all hours of the night. Today, Burton Snowboards is the largest snowboarding and gear company in the world.

Burton boards from 1977 - 1989. Notice the different shaped noses (or fronts) of the boards and the different sizes.

Snowboarders need to take good care of their boards (like this one from 1985) by tuning them and waxing the bottoms. Different waxes are used, depending on the consistency of the snow.

Sharing the Slopes

As snowboarding caught on, boarders faced a problem: where would they practice? Ski resorts weren't willing to share their hills, but snowboarders didn't give up. They practiced after dark on ski slopes and on less desirable hills with trees and bushes.

In 1981, the first snowboard (not Snurfer) competition took place. The only ski resort that allowed this sport was Ski Cooper in Colorado. A group of 12 snowboarders (including Tom Sims and Jake Burton), nicknamed the "Dirty Dozen," called the event "The King of the Mountain." Some snowboarders used homemade equipment, such as bungee cords as bindings and tennis shoes instead of snow boots.

Burton (above) in the 1980s on one of his own boards. Burton still snowboards – 100 days out of the year!

In 1982, Suicide Six Ski Area in Vermont hosted the National Snowboarding Championships, the first national snowboarding event. Snowboarders could compete in slalom runs and downhill competitions. This was the last event to have both Snurfers and snowboards in races together. Rival designers Sims and Burton raced against one another. Both are still competitors in the business and continue to make awesome boards.

Paul Sundman in the first National Snowboarding Championships in 1982. This competition still takes place today but is now called the US Open Snowboarding Championships.

39

The Styles of Snowboarding

There are lots of ways to snowboard now. Many styles overlap and people like to try out different forms. Alpine snowboarding is influenced by skiing and surfing. Freestyle snowboarding borrows from skateboarding, with boards designed for the half-pipe and for hitting jumps in the mountains. Freeriding combines elements of alpine and freestyle. Backcountry, or treeriding, happens off the trail. It uses freeride boards or split boards, which detach into separate skis so the rider can walk up the hill rather than use a ski lift. Now that there are so many different ways to enjoy the slopes on a snowboard, competitions involve more than just heading down a hill, which is how Snurfing started out.

White (left) performing at the Winter X Games in Aspen, Colorado.

Adam Moran

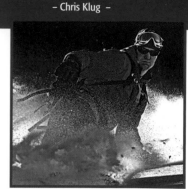

Chris Klug of Colorado in 2006 on Aspen Mountain.

Shaun White, known as the "Flying Tomato" because of his red hair, was the first to compete in the Winter and Summer X Games in two different sports. He hit the powder in the winter for snowboarding slopestyle and super-pipe and rode on wheels in the summer as a skateboarder in vert. White is seen here after learning his half-pipe score at the 2006 Olympics, where he won gold.

CP/AP/Lionel Cironneau

Going for the Gold

Snowboarding competitions are all about tricks and speed, making them appealing to a variety of people. For boarders

Snowboarders have different preferences about boards and stances. Some like to ride with their front foot facing forward; others keep both feet facing sideways.

who are into park and pipe, slopestyle is a competitive event for performing jumps on man-made, terrain-like rails. The half-pipe and super-pipe are like land sports' vertical, but in snowboarding, the ramp is made out of snow. Another competition is all about speed. Maybe you've watched skiers in the Olympics head down a hill, sliding between flags. Parallel giant slalom is a similar snowboarding event. Riders curve around flags as fast as they can without hitting one or wiping out.

Surfing started in the water, then it became a snow sport, and now even kites are used. Snow kiters (as the one seen here) ride on a snowboard or skis propelled by a kite flying in the wind.

Learn the Lingo

➤ **Fresh corduroy:** a term used by carvers when a hill has just been groomed and there are fresh lines in the snow

➤ **Freshies, and pow pow:** fresh snow

➤ **Hit:** a jump

➤ **Jibbing:** doing tricks

➤ **Jib park:** a place where rails and boxes are set up to do tricks on

➤ **Kickers:** the lip on a jump; also slang for a good jump

➤ **Nose:** the front part of the snowboard

➤ **Stomp pad:** a place on the snowboard to put the foot when getting off the chairlift

➤ **Switch:** riding backward with the opposite foot in front

When the Winter X Games first debuted in 1997, two new snowboarding events were created: boardercross and Big Air. Boardercross (or snowboard cross) gets its name from the similar motorbike event, motocross. Racers begin at the top of the course and start off at the same time, navigating down a mountain with berms (or little hills) and tabletops (flat bumps).

In the first Winter X Games, 16 women were scheduled for the women's Big Air event. Similar to water ski jump events, they would be performing one freestyle jump off a tall ramp. After looking at the jump beforehand, only four women showed up for the event. They knew that if they didn't compete, the women's division could be cut. Although they were nervous, the four went through with it, and California's Tina Basich placed third. Big Air became such a popular competition that it joined the Summer X Games too, in 1997, and required artificial snow.

Courtesy of Ian Ruhter

One of the first women to make her mark in the snowboarding world was northern California's Tina Basich (seen above, boarding in the backcountry of Canada). An amateur skateboarder, Basich began riding at age 16 when her mother bought her a snowboard she found in a ski shop. From that point on, Basich was addicted to the activity.

Adam Moran

Molly Aguirre (above) performing a handplant at Mammoth Mountain in California. In addition to competing, Aguirre also helps design boards and gear for women.

In 1998, 32 years after Snurfers were first sold, snowboarding joined the Olympics with two events: giant slalom and half-pipe. Since then, parallel giant slalom has replaced giant slalom and snowboard cross has been added. The Olympics will soon include slopestyle as well.

Dressin' Up for Cruisin' Down

Snowboarders wear practical clothing, similar to skiers: a jacket, waterproof pants, goggles, and gloves. As with other action sports, helmets are important as well. Many resorts require snowboarders to use a leash that connects the binding to the boot. A runaway board is a danger to other people on the hills.

Kelly Clark has competed in both half-pipe and boardercross.

Adam Moran

Although some will say that balancing on a snowboard is similar to balancing on snow skis, many moves come from skateboarding. Like skateboarders, snowboarders decorate their boards with graphics, both on the top sheet (or top of the board) and on the bottom.

Watching Out for Wipeouts

Although snowboarders and skiers share the hills, injuries are different. The most common injury for snowboarding involves the wrists and shoulders, because boarders break falls with their hands. Skiers are more likely to injure their legs and ankles. With both sports, there is also the risk of an avalanche on large mountains. Snowboarders should never head out to the hills alone, especially on noncommercial boarding areas.

The sport of snowboarding could have fizzled out while still called Snurfing. Instead, people around the world now enjoy the ride. So bring on the snow!

Skate In-line

Rollin' Back Through History

One of the earliest pairs of in-line skates was designed in the 1700s by Jean-Joseph Merlin of Belgium. He attached wheels in single-file rows to two small platforms. But when Merlin tried the skates, he found that he couldn't turn or stop. Even worse, he was showing his invention to a crowd while playing a violin. He crashed into a mirror, breaking the mirror and his violin.

The wheels on in-line skates have changed through the years. The bottom set of wheels are Petitbled's design from 1819. On the left are wheels from 1860. On the right are the Best-Ever-Built Skate Company's clamp-on skates from the 1930s. The booted skate is from Rollerblade In-line Skates, 1994.

National Museum of Roller Skating, Lincoln, Nebraska

The Peck & Snyder Company manufactured sporting goods, including these roller skates from 1880.

Smithsonian Institution Collections, National Museum of American History, Behring Center

Through the years, various designs were tried for skates with wheels in one straight line, but turning and stopping still weren't easy. Some skates had two wheels in a line; others had as many as six. In 1819, Monsieur Petitbled patented the first pair of roller skates in France. His pair had three wheels in a line.

Finally, in 1863, skates were designed with turning in mind. New Yorker James Plimpton, who is credited with creating the first modern roller skates, improved the skates by moving the wheels into two rows of two. This made the skates, which he called "rocker skates," more stable and more conducive to turning. Although some "in-line" skates were designed afterward, using roller skates (with two rows of wheels) became popular and stayed this way for almost 100 years.

An in-line skate from 1910 designed for roller hockey. The back wheel is higher so the skater could pivot using the center wheel.

National Museum of Roller Skating, Lincoln, Nebraska

The Olson Brothers

It was by accident that the in-line skates we know today were created. In 1979, Minnesotan Scott Olson was at a used sporting goods store and discovered an old pair of skates from 1966 with wheels all in a row. Scott and his brother, Brennan, thought they could use similar skates to practice hockey off the ice. They bought the old pair of skates and worked on improving them by adding polyurethane wheels and a heel brake. Their company, Rollerblade, was born. In 1984, Bob Naegele Jr., a Minnesota businessman, bought Rollerblade and the skates became famous. Although these weren't the first in-line skates in history, Rollerblade brand in-line skates were the first design used worldwide.

Ways to Roll

People everywhere started buckling into in-line skates for recreational use. The new skates also proved to be good training for other sports, such as snow skiing and figure skating. Soon, it was discovered that many more activities could be performed on skates:

• Freestyle skating includes "rollerdance," figure skating, and slalom. In 1997, specially designed in-line skates for figure skaters were created, complete with a urethane "toe pick" for practicing tricks off the ice. In slalom, as with other land sports that have a slalom discipline, in-line uses cones. Skaters can weave through cones forward and backward.

An aggressive skater doing a shifty over a spine ramp.

• Aggressive skating, or stunt in-line skating, attracted people who wanted to do tricks. A.J. Jackson, Pat Parnell, Doug Boyce, and Chris Morris pioneered skateboarding tricks on skates and created new in-line stunts. Performing tricks on rails, ledges, stairs, and other existing terrain is called street skating. Performing on fabricated ramps, boxes, and half-pipes is called ramp skating. Chris Edwards was one of the first skaters to try riding down a staircase rail.

• Racers can enjoy speed skating both indoors and outdoors. There are races for people who like to sprint, as well as for those who enjoy skating the distance: marathons are 26 miles and double marathons are 52.4 miles long. The current double marathon record is held by Jono Gorman from Georgia. In 2003, Gorman skated 18.41 miles per hour, finishing in two hours and 49 minutes!

In-line includes a speed skating discipline for racing. These racers (above) are on a velodrome, an arena that has a track with banked sides.

Avoiding Road Rash

Whoa, let's slow down for a minute! Safety gear is crucial for in-line skating. Luckily, the International In-line Skating Association (IISA) began in 1991 to help regulate safety rules and train in-line skating teachers. For protection, skaters should wear wrist, elbow, and knee guards and a helmet. In addition to the other safety gear, downhill skaters often wear bike shorts that have tailbone and hip "crash" pads built in.

The Olsons' original in-line skates used lightweight ski boots. Now boots are made differently for the specific type of skating being done. Recreational skate boots are usually made from a flexible plastic, while boots made for racing are leather or a combination of leather and nylon. These materials are lightweight and flexible but are still strong.

Having a Ball Skating

Q: What do you get when you combine skating with a ball?
A: Sports with a whole new kind of fun!

A roller hockey game at a skating rink in New Mexico (1996).

CP/AP-Albuquerque Journal/Jeff Alexander

Although roller hockey existed before the Olson brothers invented Rollerblades, it became more popular with the new in-line skates. Unlike ice hockey, roller hockey can be played and practiced on just about any flat surface. It was an exhibition sport at the 1992 Olympic Games in Spain.

Any basketball players out there? Tom LaGarde from Michigan played for the National Basketball Association (NBA) in the late 1970s and early 1980s. Although he loved playing basketball, his multiple knee surgeries took him out of the game. In the early 1990s, he moved to New York, where in-line skating was popular. The fun activity was easier on his knees than basketball. That's when he came up with a new idea: roller basketball. LaGarde started the National In-line Basketball League (NIBBL) in 1994. The game is played in two teams of four. Unlike traditional basketball, after a shot is made, the ball isn't thrown in from out of bounds. Instead, the players need to be ready to retrieve the ball after it has gone through the basket.

Zack Phillips from California got his inspiration for a ball-and-skate sport from kicking a pine cone down a road while skating. In 1995, Phillips organized this new game called RollerSoccer (nicknamed Zackball), using a soccer ball instead of a pine cone. It caught on, attracting enough people to hold weekly matches. Zackball is still played today.

In-line Skating Goes Downhill

In-line racing started in the 1980s, but it took another 15 years to add a hill. Downhill was first created for the 1995 X Games. Women's downhill joined the line-up the following year. Douglas Lucht from Arizona set a world record for downhill in-line skating in 1998, traveling 63 miles per hour.

Jochen Baumann

alifornian Scott Peer (above, foreground)
s the first in-line skater to help organize
nhill festivals with events in street luge,
boarding, and in-line skating.

Courtesy of StreetSki

Lucht (above, while setting the world record) wears his own design of skates called StreetSki. These in-line skates have six wheels spread out on the bottom of a flexible snow ski-like frame, and use alpine ski boots and bindings.

Learn the Lingo

➤ **Air:** jumping off something high and having space between the skater and the ground

➤ **Black ice:** what downhill in-line skaters call streets that are freshly paved

➤ **Duck walk:** walking with the skates turned out (like a duck) while having all the wheels touching the ground

➤ **Grab:** Grabbing the wheels when jumping

➤ **Handplant:** performing a handstand on a ramp

➤ **Road rash:** injuries from skating (and other sports), such as cuts and scrapes

➤ **Stair bashing:** riding on stairs

➤ **Stall:** to stop temporarily on a surface, such as a rail or coping

Counting the Wheels

Choosing a pair of in-line skates is a lot like picking out a pair of sneakers. What kind to wear depends on what type of skating someone plans on doing. Different kinds of skates have different numbers of wheels. More wheels equal more speed. Speed skates have five wheels, or four large wheels; skates for downhill usually have five or six wheels.

Aggressive in-line skates, on the other hand, usually have only four wheels since speed isn't the goal. Instead, the wheels are smaller than other types of skating wheels and flatter, so more of the wheel touches the ground. Wheels are also set up in various configurations. Sometimes only the two outer wheels touch the ground. Having flatter wheels, or a space where the smaller middle wheels are, provides more friction with surfaces that aggressive skaters grind on, such as metal railings, called "copings."

A skater performing a rocket air on the vert ramp at the Urban Games, an event that takes place in London, England.

CP/Rex Features Ltd./ Neale Haynes

Thumper Nagasako performing a hover flip at Maui Central Skate Park. Nagasako was the highest-placing American at the 2004 X Games and the highest-placing American at the 2005 World Championships.

Erik Aeder

What's Next?

What if you could skate your way through the day? It's now possible, thanks to one of the newest shoe technologies – Heelys. Like many inventors, Roger Adams, who grew up in Washington, had a "what if" idea. While watching in-line skaters at the beach, Adams wondered if shoes could be created that people could walk and roll in. In the late 1990s, he took a regular pair of sneakers, and, using a hot butter knife, cut out the heels. After that, he inserted an axle and wheel into the heel. After many tries and changes, he got his invention to work and created the first sneaker that skates. Skaters can go from walking to skating by shifting their weight from the shoe sole to the wheel. In 2000, Adams started the company Heelys, Inc. Since then, more than 10 million pairs have been sold around the world.

Heelys can change into regular sneakers by removing the wheels.

Photos courtesy of Heelys, Inc.

Adams (above) holding the size 22 shoe that Heelys made for Shaquille O'Neal.

Who knows what the next direction of in-line skating will be? With all the different sports and inspiration that have already come from in-line skating, anything is possible.

In-line skating wheels have a hardness and sturdiness scale that ranges from 1A (the softest) to 100A (the hardest). Softer wheels grip better, but harder wheels roll faster.

LOVE THE LAND OF OPPORTUNITY

Wow, America sure has a lot of talent! And each sport started so differently. Some of the groundbreakers planned their ideas in advance, others had an "aha" moment and went with it, and still others used an object in an inventive way. Regardless of how each sport started, it caught on and turned heads. It spread from one dot on the map to the rest of the country, and then the rest of the world. The activities not only have Americans moving, but they also have people in the rest of the world joining in on the fun and adding their own twists and firsts.

The modern trampoline was invented in the US and is now used in inventive ways throughout the world. "Bossaball" (above), which started in Belgium in the early 2000s, combines a bouncy surface with gymnastics, volleyball, and soccer.

Courtesy of Bossaball

Windsurfing, which combines a surfboard and sail, sprouted from surfing.

Celebrate these trendsetters, groundbreakers, and risk-takers, including the people who were behind the scenes, such as those altering the equipment, making wheels that rolled more smoothly or bike handlebars that could turn completely around in a circle. Cheer for those who got in front of the camera or tried out a new move in front of a crowd. They have shown us that sports are always changing, thanks to creative contributions, and that the possibilities are endless. Maybe these famous firsts have inspired you to learn something new. Check out your community center or local park district to see what is offered, such as skateboarding lessons or Ultimate leagues … and then get moving!

CREATE YOUR OWN FIRST!

Feeling inspired to contribute your own first? Here are some initial steps for becoming a trendsetter and groundbreaker yourself:

➤ **1. Choose somewhere to play**
Think of where you would like to play or where you would like to use a new invention. In the water? On the ground? In the air?

➤ **2. Pick an object**
Choose an object that has potential to become part of something more, such as an object with wheels or one that can fly through the air.

3. Determine a goal

What do you want to do with the object? Is it going to be part of a game with points for reaching a target? Or instead, are points awarded for style? Will it have to do with being the quickest at a task or being able to do it for the longest amount of time? Is it something done alone, in pairs, or in teams?

4. Set rules and create directions

Be sure to form rules so everyone knows in advance what is allowed. You might want to have only a few rules. Also, write directions on how to use the equipment. After trying your invention a couple of times, you may think of new rules and directions, or you may need to change them.

5. Stay safe

Remember that the most important thing is to stay safe. Always wear necessary protective gear, such as a helmet or knee pads. Be sure that an adult approves the activity and is close by to help. The tricks and moves in this book are not meant for you to try. They can be dangerous and should be attempted only by experts with proper training, safety equipment, and supervision.

6. Share it

Each of the people in this book who tried something new followed one of the fundamental rules of creation: don't keep it a secret! Just think what would have happened if the groundbreakers within these pages had decided to keep their breakthroughs to themselves. Greats like Tony Hawk, Kelly Slater, and Shaun White might not be household names if it weren't for Larry Stevenson, Alexander Hume Ford, and Sherman Poppen. Luckily these famous firsts shared their ideas, and, as a result, we can now enjoy some pretty cool things. So show off your new idea to others. They might have creative ideas to contribute as well.

7. Have fun!

Have a good time and inspire others to do the same!

DID YOU KNOW...

...that in 1976, Dale Webster, a California surfer, began a 10,407-day surfing marathon? Webster started his journey on February 29th of that leap year and wanted to surf every day until the next time that February 29th fell on the fifth Sunday of February – 28 years later. Webster did it, surfing at least three waves every single day until February 29, 2004, regardless of the weather or his mood. Now that's a committed surfer!

...that four US presidents were once cheerleaders? Franklin D. Roosevelt was a cheerleader at Harvard College; Dwight D. Eisenhower cheered for West Point Academy; Ronald Reagan was a cheerleader at Eureka College; and George W. Bush was part of the cheerleading squad at Phillips Academy. Let's hear it for the red, white, and blue!

George W. Bush in his cheerleading days at Phillips Academy, 1964. Courtesy of Phillips Academy

Continued on p. 48